In the beginning God
the heaven a

Living things ran on the earth
and flew in the skies,
and swam in the seas.
And God saw that it was
good.

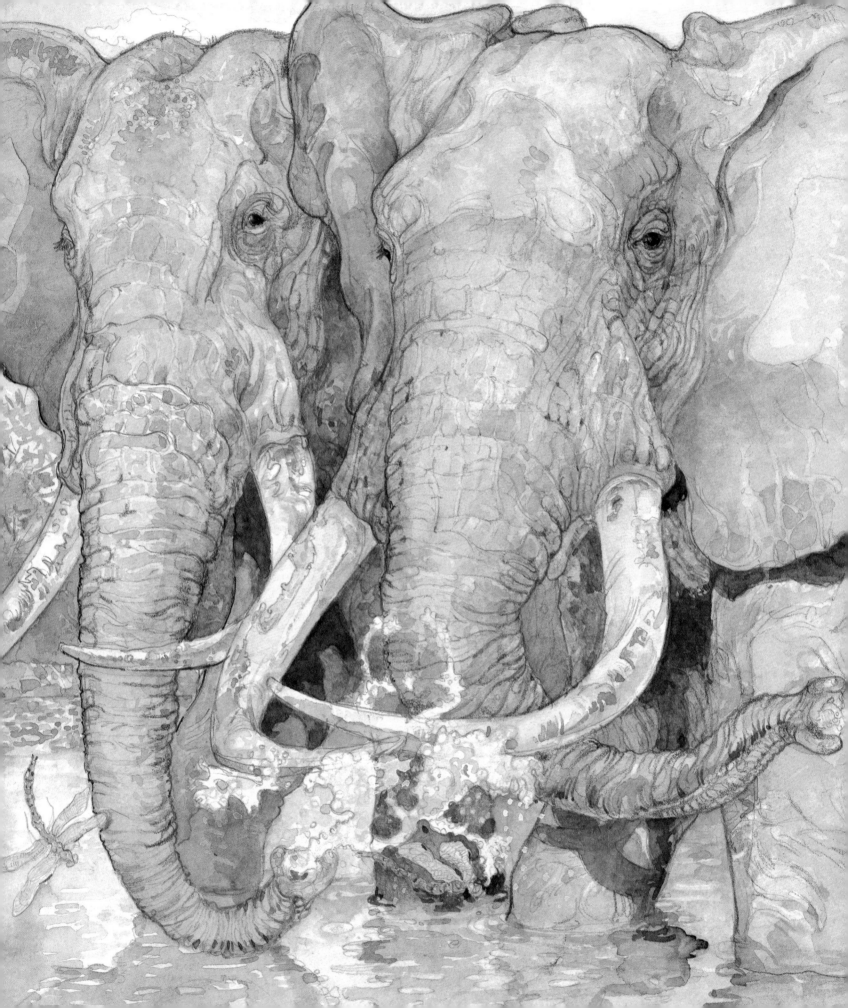

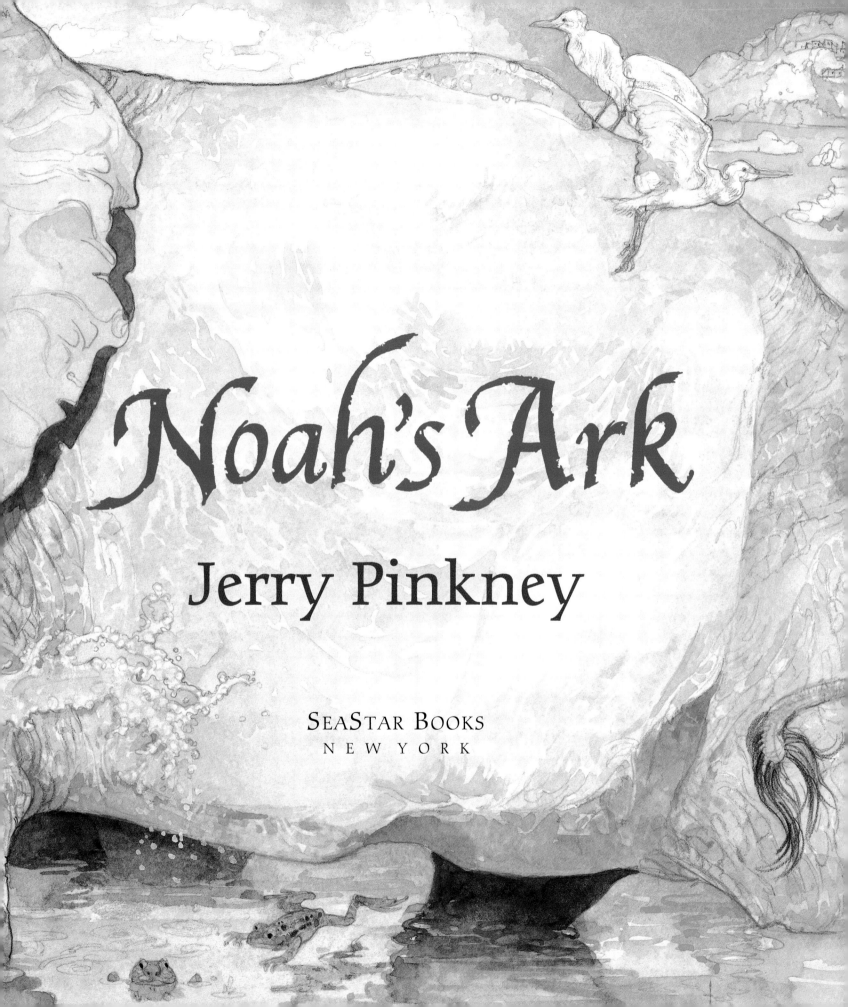

Noah's Ark

Jerry Pinkney

SeaStar Books
NEW YORK

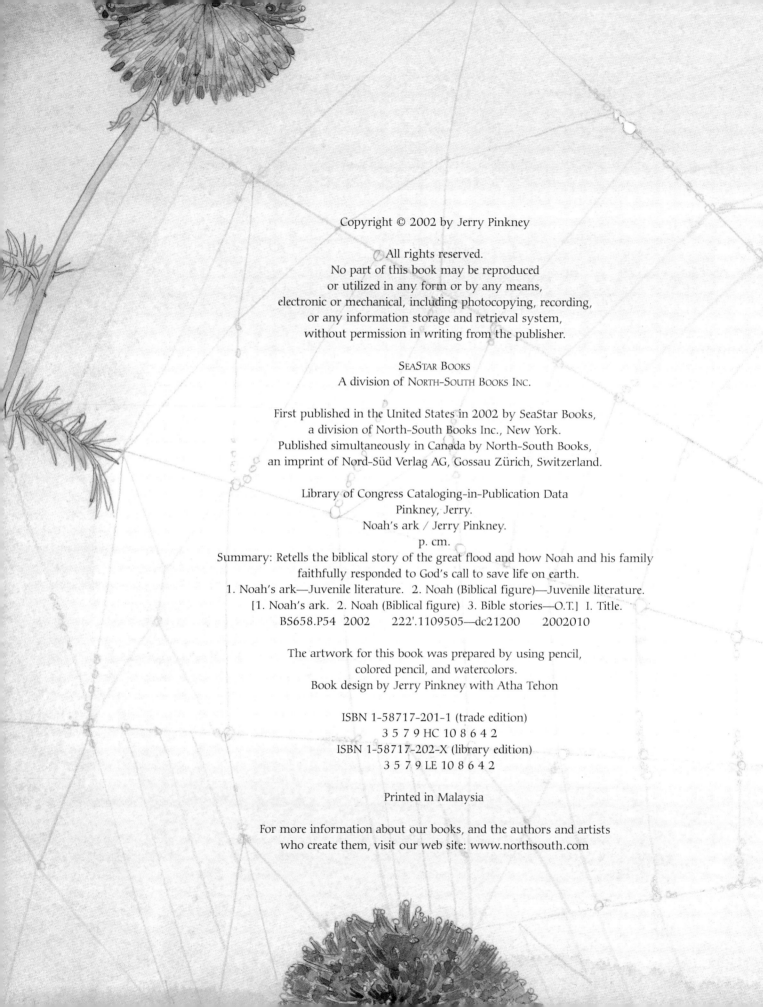

SeaStar Books
A division of North-South Books Inc.

First published in the United States in 2002 by SeaStar Books,
a division of North-South Books Inc., New York.
Published simultaneously in Canada by North-South Books,
an imprint of Nord-Süd Verlag AG, Gossau Zürich, Switzerland.

Library of Congress Cataloging-in-Publication Data
Pinkney, Jerry.
Noah's ark / Jerry Pinkney.
p. cm.
Summary: Retells the biblical story of the great flood and how Noah and his family
faithfully responded to God's call to save life on earth.
1. Noah's ark—Juvenile literature. 2. Noah (Biblical figure)—Juvenile literature.
[1. Noah's ark. 2. Noah (Biblical figure) 3. Bible stories—O.T.] I. Title.
BS658.P54 2002   222'.1109505—dc21200   2002010

The artwork for this book was prepared by using pencil,
colored pencil, and watercolors.
Book design by Jerry Pinkney with Atha Tehon

ISBN 1-58717-201-1 (trade edition)
3 5 7 9 HC 10 8 6 4 2
ISBN 1-58717-202-X (library edition)
3 5 7 9 LE 10 8 6 4 2

Printed in Malaysia

For more information about our books, and the authors and artists
who create them, visit our web site: www.northsouth.com

To the caretakers of all things,
big and small
J. P.

God was not pleased
with the people of the earth.
They did not care for one another.
They did not care for the land that God had made.
And they did not care for God.

God's heart was filled with pain
to see the wickedness of humankind.
God decided to sweep away
all living things on the earth.

But Noah did what was right
in the sight of the Lord.
And the Lord loved Noah.

God spoke to Noah.
Noah put down his basket and listened.
God said,
"Make an ark out of cypress wood.
For I am going to bring a great flood upon the earth,
and it will swallow up every living thing."

God said,
"Bring two of every creature on the ark.
Bring food for them and for yourself.
I make this promise to you:
you and your family
and the animals that you bring with you
will be safe."

Noah did as the Lord commanded.
His family helped him build the ark.
Every day it rose higher and higher.

It rose over their heads.
It rose over the treetops.
The strong wooden beams
embraced the clouds.

At last the ark was done.
Noah filled baskets with grain.
His wife baked loaves of bread.
His three sons gathered grapes and olives.
His sons' wives poured water into jars
and carried them to the ark
to fill it with food
for every living thing.

People came to stare at the ark
as it sat on the top of a hill.
"What fool builds a ship
on dry land?" they cried.
"The ocean is miles away!"
But Noah trusted in the Lord.
And the clouds began to gather.

God called to the animals,
and from aardvark to zebra they came.
The deer bounded through the tall grass.
The elephants ran
and it sounded like thunder.
The wings of the birds
cast a shadow on the earth.

Two by two they came,
all the animals of the earth.
They came to the ark where Noah waited.
And Noah welcomed them.

They followed him into the ark,
and God closed the door behind them.

The rains began.
The lakes and rivers and creeks and streams
overflowed their banks.
The oceans rose.
Slowly the water crept over the land,
higher and higher.

The water rose over cities and towns.
Whales swam down ruined streets.
Schools of fish darted through empty windows.

But God remembered Noah and his family
and all the animals on the ark.
The ark floated on the waters.
Everyone inside was safe.

The zebras munched their hay.
The geese gobbled up the grain.
The monkeys nibbled on sweet grapes
and climbed to the roof
where the sparrows
perched and sang.

After forty days and forty nights
the rain stopped falling.
God sent a great wind over the earth.
And slowly, slowly,
the waters began to go down.

At last the ark came to rest
on the top of the highest mountain.
But all around
there was nothing but water.

Noah opened a window
and sent out a raven
to fly over the face
of the waters.
But the raven found
no dry land.

Noah sent out a dove
to fly over the waters.
But the dove found no dry land.

Noah had faith in God,
and he sent the dove again.
The dove returned to Noah
with an olive branch in its beak.
Then Noah knew
that there was dry land at last.

Slowly, slowly, the waters went down.
Slowly, the earth dried.
The sun shone again. The grass grew.
At last it was time to leave the ark.

The owls and the eagles
spread their wings and soared.
The panther sprang to the soft ground.
The grasshoppers leapt
and the lizards scurried.
Noah and his family
turned their faces up to the sun
and sang praise to God.

Noah and his family
planted seeds for the first harvest.
They cared for the earth that God had made.

God said,
"Never again will I send a flood
upon the earth to destroy it.
From this day forward,
life on earth will grow and prosper."

And God
set a rainbow in the heavens
as a sign of this promise to Noah
and to Noah's family
and to every living thing.

Seedtime and harvest, cold and heat
summer and winter,
night and day,
shall never cease
as long as the earth
endures.